The Dig

Dig In • Find the Treasure • Put it on Display

Volume 2 • Luke 13 – 24

Patrick Schwenk

www.thedigforkids.com

ISBN-13: 978-0-615-77457-2

Table of Contents

A Word to Parents

Hello, and welcome to *The Dig*!

I am a pastor, husband, and parent. Currently, my wife and I have four children ten years old and younger. My wife and I clean up spills, refill drinks, do laundry, change diapers, cut the grass, serve in ministry, drop kids off, pick kids up, take out the trash, clean the house, do more laundry – you get the point!

Like you, my wife and I wear many hats. One of the greatest joys in my life is being a dad and having the pleasure to be a pastor to my kids. My daughter said to me recently, "Dad, I am glad you are a pastor." When I asked her why, she said, "Because you teach us the Bible."

The truth is, every parent should be (and can be) a pastor to his or her children. *The Dig* has been my personal desire and attempt to teach our children the Bible from an early age.

The Apostle Paul makes an interesting comment regarding Timothy's training as a child. In 2 Timothy 3:14-15, Paul says, "But as for you, continue in what you have learned and have firmly believed, knowing from whom you learned it and **how from childhood you have been acquainted with the sacred writings,** which are able to make you wise for salvation through faith in Christ Jesus."

Paul suggests that Timothy was being taught the Bible from a very young age. *The Dig* is an effort to systematically help you as a parent study through books of the Bible so you can help your child. Out of the experience you create, biblical principles are learned and lived.

The goal, of course, is that our children will fall in love with Jesus as their Savior and grow up to follow Him with all their heart, soul, and strength. I trust that this will be a great resource for you and your family!

In Jesus,

Patrick Schwenk

About Discipleship

Before we get too far into *The Dig*, let's look at a few brief observations about teaching and training our children to be disciples of Jesus.

1. We must have the **RIGHT PICTURE** of who we want our children to be. Close your eyes for a moment and picture your son or daughter when they are 15, 25, or 35 years old. What do they look like? What do they care about? How do they pray? How do they worship? Whom do they love? As Christian parents, if the picture of our children is anything other than a disciple of Jesus, then we are aiming at the wrong target. The goal is to raise children who live, love, and serve like Jesus!

2. We must have the **RIGHT PRIORITIES**. The right picture helps us establish the right priorities. What is important to you as a parent? What do you push your children to get involved in? Why? What does success look like for you as a parent? What does success look like for your child? One of the great joys of being a parent is having the opportunity to raise children who love God. This doesn't happen by accident. It is by God's grace and our own effort to establish godly priorities.

3. We must have the **RIGHT PERSPECTIVE**. It is still God's grace that saves our children and not our best intentions or methods. With this said, keep in mind the following:

   Information: Children are oftentimes growing up in American churches and homes less biblically literate than the previous generations. As parents, we need to be reminded of the tremendous responsibility we have to pass on the truth of God's Word.

   Impression: The goal is also to leave a positive spiritual impression on the hearts of our children. Our children won't have a pleasant memory if all they remember is Mom or Dad (tired and grouchy) drilling Bible verses into their heads! Taking your child through *The Dig* should be a memorable experience. Best lessons are taught within the context of loving and meaningful relationships.

   Imitation: Don't forget that our children listen to us and watch us. As a parent, we must be growing as a disciple of Jesus ourselves. We want to be able to say, as Paul did to the church in Corinth, "Follow me as I follow Christ" (I Corinthians 11:1).

About *The Dig*

Shortly, you will meet a character named Doc. Doc is an experienced Bible scholar and archaeologist who will be your *Dig* tour guide during each lesson. A typical *Dig* lesson follows the same pattern consisting of four main parts. Below is a short description of each of these four components.

1. **The Map**: Each lesson has a map. The map tells you and your child where you'll be going in each lesson. It is a short summary of the study ahead.

2. **The Dig**: The Dig is the main passage you will be studying. Following each passage will be several questions designed to help conversation and understanding. They are meant to be a guide. You can use them or tweak them to help you talk with your children.

3. **The Treasure**: The Treasure is the big idea of the lesson. In a short statement, it is what you want your child to remember from the passage you studied.

4. **The Display**: When an archaeologist finds a treasure, they will clean it up and put in on display for everyone to see. This is the basic idea of the Display. It is the application of the Treasure you have found. This is a great opportunity to discuss with your child how he or she can live out the truth of God's Word for everyone to see.

The Oasis is a chance to review what your child has learned so far. Make it your own and make it fun. A quiz and coloring activity are provided, and you can provide the prize! You'll also notice there are key verses in each section. Memorizing God's Word is a great way to hide God's Word in the heart of your child and also to reinforce what your son or daughter is learning.

Enjoy the adventure!

Introduction to Luke

Greetings!

Welcome back! Most likely you have already completed Volume 1 and are now ready for the next adventure through Volume 2. As you know, I'm Doc! I've been studying the Bible, history, and archaeology for a long time. I love to learn about God's Word and teach others, too. I am very excited you are joining me on this Bible adventure through the second part of the Gospel of Luke. Since you most likely know some things about Luke, the following is for your review.

Who is the author?

With God's help, Luke wrote one of the books in the New Testament that we call the Gospel of Luke. Most Bible experts believe that Luke, who was a doctor and follower of Jesus, wrote this book to make sure all the facts were right about who Jesus is and what Jesus did.

Would you be mad if someone was telling other people things about you that were not true? I would be very upset! Luke wanted to make sure this didn't happen to Jesus. He wrote the Gospel of Luke so that everyone would know what was really true about Jesus.

Take a minute and see if you can find the book of Luke in your Bible. Did you find it? The first four books in the New Testament are called the gospels. They tell us about who Jesus is and what He did. The third gospel is Luke and it is the book you'll be studying again very shortly. Soon, you will be a Bible expert, too!

What is the date?

Do you know when you were born? I was born in 1975. Wow, I know that is long time ago! Well, Luke wrote this book around the year 60 A.D. Now that is a really long time ago! God wanted to make sure we would never forget what He has done, so He helped people write the Bible.

Are you ready for an adventure through the rest of the Gospel of Luke? I am! Let's pray and get ready to check out our first **map**, go on a **dig**, find our **treasure**, and put God's Word on **display**!

Let's dig,

Doc

Lesson 1:
Turn Around

Key Verse: Luke 13:29

And people will come from east and west, and from north and south, and recline at table in the kingdom of God.

The Map:

Hiking in Israel can be dangerous. If you aren't careful, going down the wrong path can lead you to the edge of a cliff instead of to the top of a mountain. If you are heading in the wrong direction, you better turn around and head in the right direction! We're going to look at a passage where Jesus warns people to turn, or repent, from the direction they are going and follow Him. Don't forget to start memorizing your key verse. It is Luke 13:29.

The Dig: Luke 13:1-9

What does Jesus say we need to do if we are sinning?

What does it mean to repent?

What does Jesus say about the fig tree? Does it have any fruit on it?

The Treasure:

Turn from sin and turn to Jesus! Because God loves us and knows what is best for us, He wants us to listen and obey Him. Sometimes we need to turn, or repent, from our sins and turn back to loving and obeying Jesus.

The Display:

Jesus teaches us that if we are living for God we will be like a fig tree that is growing good fruit. What kind of "fruit" does Jesus want us to have in our lives? Take a moment and read Galatians 5:22-23.

Lesson 2:
Help, I'm Hurting

Key Verse: Luke 13:29

And people will come from east and west, and from north and south, and recline at table in the kingdom of God.

The Map:

Have you ever helped someone who was hurting? I remember being in Tel Aviv almost twenty years ago when a man was left stranded on the side of the road because he had run out of gas. People kept driving by him without stopping to help. In this lesson, we'll learn how Jesus helped a woman by healing her while others stood around not wanting to help.

The Dig: Luke 13:10-17

On what day is Jesus teaching in the synagogue? Do you remember what the Sabbath is?

What is wrong with the woman who is there?

What are the Jewish religious leaders doing? Why do you think they aren't helping her?

What does Jesus do?

The Treasure:

Help the hurting! Each day you may have friends or even a brother or sister who needs your help. While the religious leaders stood around, Jesus did something for the woman who needed help. He didn't ignore those around him who were hurting.

The Display:

Can you think of people around you that may be going through a tough time? What are some ways you could help people who are hurting?

Lesson 3:
Little Is Big in God's Eyes

Key Verse: Luke 13:29

And people will come from east and west, and from north and south, and recline at table in the kingdom of God.

The Map:

In this lesson, we'll be looking at how small things grow into big things for God! Jesus is going to use the example of a tiny mustard seed and yeast to teach us a very valuable lesson. Let's dig!

The Dig: Luke 13:18-21

Jesus uses two examples in this passage. What are they?

How do both of these things, the seed and the yeast, start out? Are they big or small?

What does the seed grow into?

What happens to the yeast?

The Treasure:

Little things done for God can turn into something big! Have you ever seen a small seed? A seed might start out small, but as it grows, it eventually becomes something much bigger. Some things we do for God might seem small. There may even be times when we obey God and nobody is around to see it. But obedience, even in small things, can make big changes in the world!

The Display:

Take a moment and list a few things that might seem like small things. How could these small things make big changes in the world?

Lesson 4:
The Narrow Door

Key Verse: Luke 13:29

And people will come from east and west, and from north and south, and recline at table in the kingdom of God.

The Map:

There is a large mountain fortress in Israel called Masada. It is very close to the Dead Sea. It was built by King Herod and then later used by the Romans. One day we were digging for artifacts on top of Masada. As we were leaving, we came across two doors. We knew one door took us outside the fortress, but the other one led deep into the ground where they used to store water. Choosing the right door was very important! This lesson deals with two doors and choosing wisely. Let's dig!

The Dig: Luke 13:22-30

What question do people ask Jesus at the beginning of this passage?

Which door does Jesus tell them to enter? Will people be able to enter through the door after it is closed?

Look at verse 29 again. Where will people come from to be a part of this big party, or feast, in Heaven?

The Treasure:

Jesus is the only way to Heaven! We are not saved by the good things we do. We are saved by our faith in Jesus. He is the door we must enter to go to Heaven one day! Jesus is teaching us that He is the Way. He doesn't want us to wait to trust in Him.

The Display:

God created you and loves you. He wants you to believe in Him as your Savior. Why do you think we need a Savior? Have you ever prayed and asked Jesus to be your Savior? Do you have friends you can pray for who aren't Christians?

Lesson 5:
Crying Over Jerusalem

Key Verse: Luke 13:29

And people will come from east and west, and from north and south, and recline at table in the kingdom of God.

The Map:

Do you know someone who cries a lot? Well, the Bible tells us that Jesus cried, too! He didn't cry because He got in trouble or because someone didn't give Him what He wanted. In this lesson, we'll learn about how Jesus cried for the people in Jerusalem because they had not turned to Him to be saved from their sins.

The Dig: Luke 13:31-35

What do some of the Pharisees tell Jesus to do?

Even though Herod wants to kill Jesus, does it stop Him?

Why is Jesus so sad for the people of Jerusalem?

The Treasure:

Jesus wept for people who were unwilling to come to Him as their Savior. Jesus loved people so much that it made Him sad when He knew that there were some who wouldn't believe in Him as the Messiah, God's Savior. It broke His heart because He had come to help them and save them. He knew the time was running out for them to turn to Him and be forgiven of their sins.

The Display:

Jesus has a big heart for people! Not only did He care about those who were His disciples, but He also cared for those who had not yet believed in Him. How can you show love for family or friends who aren't Christians? Are there people you know who don't believe in Jesus yet that you can begin praying for?

Lesson 6:
The Great or the Grateful?

Key Verse: Luke 13:29

And people will come from east and west, and from north and south, and recline at table in the kingdom of God.

The Map:

Several years ago I had the chance to meet with the greatest archaeologist in the world. We were both going to be in Israel working on a dig in the same city. I was so excited because I actually got to eat lunch with him! Jesus is going to teach us a very important lesson about who belongs with Him. Let's dig!

The Dig: Luke 14:1-14

Look at verse 8 again. Where does Jesus say not to sit?

Take another look at verse 10. Where does Jesus say that the invited should sit?

What does Jesus say will happen to the humble? If you need a hint, look at verse 11.

The Treasure:

Jesus loves the humble! Some people think they are great because of what they know or what they can do. Jesus is teaching us that we should not focus on how great we think we are, but keep our eyes on how great God is. A humble person thinks more about God and others than they do about themselves.

The Display:

Being humble doesn't mean you never think about yourself. It just means you think about others and God more often. What are ways you can think about others first?

The Oasis

Congratulations! You have made it through the first six lessons. The Oasis is a chance to stop, rest up, and review what you have learned so far on the adventure. During each Oasis, you will be quizzed over the lessons you have already done. Do you think you can remember what you have studied so far? Let's find out!

Review Key Verse: Luke 13:29

Take a minute and tell your mom or dad the key verse. Remember, you are not allowed to look!

Review Questions:

1. What does it mean to repent?

2. Which door does Jesus say people should enter?

3. Jesus tells several stories about the Kingdom of God. Do you remember where He says people would come from to eat at the big party or feast?

4. Why is Jesus so sad for the people of Jerusalem?

5. In Luke 14, we hear where Jesus tells people not to sit when they throw a party. Do you remember what seat it is?

6. What does it mean to be humble?

The Oasis Activity

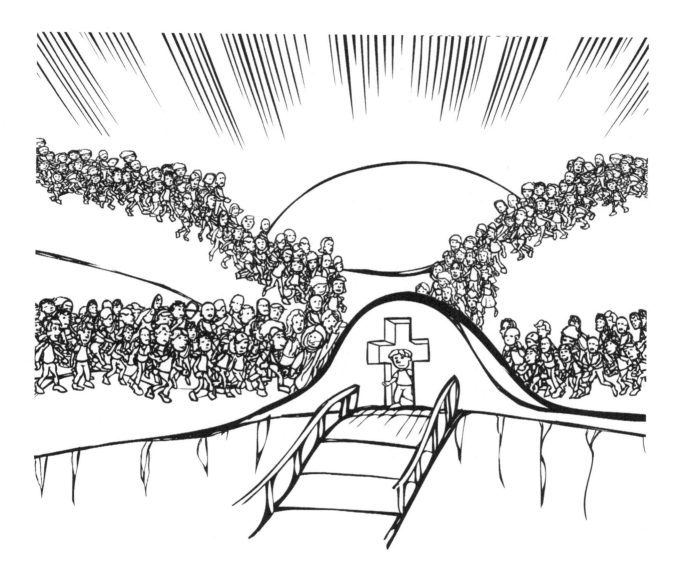

PEOPLE WILL COME FROM EAST AND WEST AND NORTH AND SOUTH, AND
WILL TAKE THEIR PLACES AT THE FEAST IN THE KINGDOM OF GOD. DRAW
WHAT YOU THINK THE FEAST WILL LOOK LIKE.

Lesson 7:
You're Invited

Key Verse: Luke 15:10

Just so, I tell you, there is joy before the angels of God
over one sinner who repents.

The Map:

In this lesson, we'll be looking at a story Jesus tells about an invitation to a party. Have you ever been invited to someone's party? Were you excited to go? Unfortunately, not everyone who is invited to the party Jesus is talking about will go. Don't forget to start memorizing your next key verse. It is Luke 15:10. Let's dig!

The Dig: Luke 14:15-24

In the story Jesus is telling, what is the man preparing? If you need a hint, look at verse 16 again.

Does he invite a lot of people?

What do some of the people who are invited do?

Who does the man invite next? Look at verse 21.

The Treasure:

Jesus wants others to join Him! In the Old Testament, God's people, the Israelites, pictured Heaven as a big feast or party. Check out Isaiah 25:6. Unfortunately, some people will make excuses and not want to join God. Others will be excited that God loves them so much to invite them to His party!

The Display:

Jesus tells this story to show that all kinds of people are welcomed by God. How do you show other kids they are loved by God and welcomed by you, too?

Lesson 8:
Hard, but Worth It

Key Verse: Luke 15:10

Just so, I tell you, there is joy before the angels of God
over one sinner who repents.

The Map:

There are a lot of mountains and hills in Israel. It can be hot, dusty, and kind of dangerous at times hiking up trails. It might be hard work, but it is a great adventure! In this lesson, we'll read how Jesus teaches us that following Him can be the same way. It's not always easy, but it is worth it! It can be a real adventure to live for God. Let's dig!

The Dig: Luke 14:25-34

Does Jesus say we are supposed to hate our family to follow Him? (Don't get too worried; I will explain what Jesus means!)

What is the man who is building the tower supposed to do before he builds?

What is the man who is going to war supposed to do before he goes into battle?

The Treasure:

Love everything less than Jesus! Don't worry; Jesus isn't saying we should hate our family. The Bible teaches that we should honor and respect our parents. When Jesus says "hate," it means to "love less." What Jesus is saying is that we should love everything else less than we love Him. He should be number one!

The Display:

Sometimes it's not easy to follow Jesus, but because we love Him so much, we know that it is worth it! Can you think of some times when it is hard to follow Jesus? Why do you think following Jesus is worth it, even when it's hard?

Lesson 9:
Lost

Key Verse: Luke 15:10

Just so, I tell you, there is joy before the angels of God
over one sinner who repents.

The Map:

Have you ever lost something you really liked? How did you feel? In Luke 15, Jesus is going to tell three parables, or stories, about losing something. The first two parables are about a lost sheep and a lost coin. Let's take a look!

The Dig: Luke 15:1-10

Who is gathered around listening to this parable? Look at verses 1 and 2 if you need a hint.

What are the Pharisees saying?

How many sheep are lost in this story?

What happens when the sheep and the coin are found in these two parables?

The Treasure:

God loves sinners! The point of these two parables is that God wants to love us and forgive us of our sins. The Pharisees in this story didn't think they needed to be forgiven. We don't have to pretend like we don't sin because God loves us!

The Display:

Even after we become a Christian, we still sin sometimes. Check out 1 John 1:8-9. The word "confess" means to admit to God what we have done wrong. Are there some things you need to confess to God, or ask Him to help you with?

Lesson 10:
Loving Father

Key Verse: Luke 15:10

Just so, I tell you, there is joy before the angels of God
over one sinner who repents.

The Map:

Jesus has already told us two parables about a lost sheep and a lost coin. In this lesson, we'll learn about a lost son who returned home, but most importantly, returned to his loving father. Let's dig!

The Dig: Luke 15:11-32

What did the youngest son ask his father for?

Where did the youngest son go?

What happens to the youngest son when he is gone?

What does his father do when he returns?

The Treasure:

God is full of grace! Grace is receiving God's love when we don't deserve it. The father did not have to forgive the youngest son's sins and welcome him home, but he did! This is how God the Father acts towards sinners who turn away from their sins and turn to Jesus.

The Display:

Aren't you glad that God is willing to forgive us when we sin? I know I am! Not only does God show love and forgiveness toward us, but He wants us to show love and forgiveness towards others, too. How do you usually treat people if they make you mad? Can you think of some examples of how we can show love and forgiveness?

Lesson 11:
Generosity or Greed?

Key Verse: Luke 15:10

Just so, I tell you, there is joy before the angels of God
over one sinner who repents.

The Map:

Have you ever had to borrow money from a friend or family member? Imagine if you needed to borrow $1 and they charged you another $3 just for loaning you the money! That wouldn't be too fair, would it? This is what is going on in the parable we are about to read. Let's dig!

The Dig: Luke 16:1-15

In this story, Jesus mentions the master, the manager, and the debtors. What did the manager do for the debtors who owed money? Look at verses 5 – 7.

Was the master happy he did this?

What does Jesus say you cannot serve?

Which group of religious leaders was Jesus talking to in this parable? Look at verse 14.

The Treasure:

The manager in this story was charging people extra money. Even though this was very mean, he did it because he loved money more than doing what was right. Jesus isn't saying it's wrong to have money. He is teaching that we should never love money more than God. God is our treasure!

The Display:

Do you know what it means to be greedy? That was the problem in this story. Jesus wants His disciples to be generous. What are some ways you can be generous with what God has given you?

Lesson 12:
Marriage Matters

Key Verse: Luke 15:10

Just so, I tell you, there is joy before the angels of God
over one sinner who repents.

The Map:

My mom and dad got married a long time ago. In fact, they have been married for 49 years. That is a long time! I know you are a long way away from getting married, but in this lesson, we'll learn about how God created marriage and why it matters.

The Dig: Luke 16:16-18

Which two people in the Bible were the first to get married? Take a look at what Jesus says in Mark 10:6-9.

Who does Jesus say marriage is for?

In Mark 10:9, Jesus says that marriage is when a man and a woman are joined together as one. What does He say a married couple should try really hard to not let happen?

The Treasure:

Marriage matters, so stay together! During Jesus' time, some of the husbands were not treating their wives very well. Instead of staying together, they were separating. Jesus was reminding them that God really wants a husband and a wife to be faithful to one another in marriage.

The Display:

Being a mom and dad is hard! Tonight, before you go to bed, write a note to your mom and dad telling them how much you love them and appreciate all they do.

The Oasis

Congratulations! You have made it through the next six lessons! The Oasis is a chance to stop, rest up, and review what you have learned so far on the adventure. During each Oasis, you will be quizzed over the lessons you have already done. Do you think you can remember what you have studied so far? Let's find out!

Review Key Verse: Luke 15:10

Take a minute and tell your mom or dad the key verse. Remember, you are not allowed to look!

Review Questions:

1. In Lesson 7, we learned about how there will be a great feast or party in Heaven. Did everyone come who was invited?

2. What do some of the people who are invited do?

3. In Lesson 8, we learned about a man who was building a tower. What is he supposed to do before building?

4. In Luke 15, Jesus told three parables about something that was lost and then found. What are those three things?

5. In the story of the son who ran away from home, what does the father do when he sees his son returning?

6. How would you explain God's grace?

The Oasis Activity

THIS WOMAN HAS TEN SILVER COINS. SHE KNOWS WHERE NINE OF THEM ARE, BUT ONE IS LOST. CAN YOU FIND AND COLOR ALL TEN?

Lesson 13:
The Rich Man

Key Verse: Luke 18:16

But Jesus called them to him, saying, "Let the children come to me, and do not hinder them, for to such belongs the kingdom of God."

The Map:

In this lesson, we'll read a sad story about two men who die. One is very rich and the other is very poor. The rich man thought he had everything he needed. The only problem was that he didn't have God. Don't forget to start memorizing your next key verse. It is Luke 18:16. Let's dig!

The Dig: Luke 16:19-31

How does Jesus describe the rich man in verse 19?

How does Jesus describe the beggar in verses 20 and 21?

What happens to both of them in this parable?

What does the rich man want to do?

The Treasure:

Don't leave God out of your life! Even though the rich man thought he had it all, he didn't have God. He thought his possessions were more important than loving and obeying God.

The Display:

The Bible teaches that we should use what God has given us to help others in need. What are some ways you can help those around you?

Lesson 14:
Be Forgiving

Key Verse: Luke 18:16

But Jesus called them to him, saying, "Let the children come to me, and do not hinder them,
for to such belongs the kingdom of God."

The Map:

Several years ago I had to leave a dig I was working on in Turkey to go to Egypt. Before I left, I made sure the archaeologist I was working with was ready to continue the work when I was gone. As Jesus is heading to Jerusalem, He is going to be teaching about making sure His disciples are ready once He is gone!

The Dig: Luke 17:1-10

What is Jesus warning His disciples not to do in verse 1?

If someone sins against us, what does Jesus say we are supposed to do?

Take a look at Ephesians 4:32. Why are we supposed to forgive other people?

The Treasure:

Be forgiving because you have been forgiven! It is not easy to forgive someone when they sin against us. But Jesus is teaching us that just as God has forgiven us, we should be willing to forgive others. Because God loves us, we can love others!

The Display:

Describe a time when someone did something to you that you didn't like. What did you do? Take a few minutes and discuss how you can show forgiveness when someone sins against you.

Lesson 15:
Be Thankful

Key Verse: Luke 18:16

But Jesus called them to him, saying, "Let the children come to me, and do not hinder them, for to such belongs the kingdom of God."

The Map:

Have you ever had someone do something really nice for you? I'll bet you thanked them! In this lesson, we'll see what Jesus has to say about being thankful for what God has done.

The Dig: Luke 17:11-19

In verse 11, where is Jesus traveling?

Who calls out to Jesus?

What does He tell them to do?

How many return to thank Him?

The Treasure:

The forgetful are never thankful! Out of the ten men who were healed, only one came back praising God. How quickly the other nine forgot what God had done for them. We need to constantly remember all that God has done for us. Remembering God's love will keep us thankful!

The Display:

It's easy to forget about how amazing God is. When we forget how He loves us, saved us, leads us, and provides for us, we stop being thankful. What are a few things you are most thankful to God for?

Lesson 16:
Be Ready

Key Verse: Luke 18:16

But Jesus called them to him, saying, "Let the children come to me, and do not hinder them, for to such belongs the kingdom of God."

The Map:

When I travel to Israel, I always fly out of the Tel Aviv airport. Like a lot of airports, it is pretty big. I always like to get there early to make sure I am ready. In this lesson, we'll learn about what Jesus has to say about being ready. Let's dig!

The Dig: Luke 17:20-37

The Jewish people during Jesus' day were waiting for God to save them from their enemies. Does Jesus say we will know exactly when He will return?

What does He say it will be like when He returns? If you need a hint, look again at verse 24.

What two examples does Jesus use? Note that He mentions two stories from the Old Testament.

Does Jesus say everyone will be ready when He returns?

The Treasure:

Don't just watch for Jesus – work for Jesus! The Bible teaches that when Jesus returns there will be no more death, pain, sickness, or suffering. What an awesome day that will be! Jesus is teaching that we are to be ready for His return.

The Display:

We don't know when Jesus will return. It could be tomorrow, or it could be in 100 years! Nobody but God knows for sure. What are you looking forward to the most when Jesus returns? How are some ways we can live to be ready for His return?

Lesson 17:
Constant Prayer

Key Verse: Luke 18:16

But Jesus called them to him, saying, "Let the children come to me, and do not hinder them, for to such belongs the kingdom of God."

The Map:

I have traveled to some pretty scary places in the world, but one thing I always do is pray! In this lesson, we'll be looking at what Jesus says about praying and never giving up. Are you ready to dig?

The Dig: Luke 18:1-8

Why does Jesus tell this parable to His disciples? Look again at verse 1.

Jesus tells a story about a judge who is not very nice. What does the widow keep doing?

Does the judge listen to her?

How is God different than the judge in this story?

The Treasure:

Never give up on God because He doesn't give up on you! Jesus tells this story to teach His disciples to never give up. Unlike the judge, God is a loving Father who cares about His children. He is always listening, so keep on coming to Him in prayer!

The Display:

Prayer is talking to God. It doesn't have to be fancy and it doesn't have to be only for special times. You can pray anytime and anywhere! What are some things you need to pray about now?

Lesson 18:
Humble Prayer

Key Verse: Luke 18:16

But Jesus called them to him, saying, "Let the children come to me, and do not hinder them, for to such belongs the kingdom of God."

The Map:

Two years ago I met the director of a museum in France. He is very well-known and important. The problem is that he wants everyone else to know how great he is! We're going to read a story that Jesus tells about someone who wanted other people and God to know how great he thought he was. Let's dig!

The Dig: Luke 18:9-17

Who is Jesus telling this story to? Take a look at verse 9.

What does the Pharisee say about himself in his prayer?

What does the tax collector say to God in his prayer?

Which man is accepted, or justified, by God?

The Treasure:

God is great! The Pharisee thought he was someone great, but the tax collector knew that he was a sinner in need of God's love and forgiveness. Some people think they are justified or loved by God because of their good behavior. We know we need God because we are not perfect!

The Display:

God wants us to come to Him not because we're great, but because He is. He always promises to love us and forgive us when we sin. What do you need to ask God to help you with?

The Oasis

Congratulations! You have made it through the next six lessons! The Oasis is a chance to stop, rest up, and review what you have learned so far on the adventure. During each Oasis, you will be quizzed over the lessons you have already done. Do you think you can remember what you have studied so far? Let's find out!

Review Key Verse: Luke 18:16

Take a minute and tell your mom or dad the key verse. Remember, you are not allowed to look!

Review Questions:

1. What does Jesus teach His disciples to do if they are sinned against?

2. How many lepers does Jesus heal?

3. How many come back praising and thanking God?

4. Does the unjust judge listen to the widow?

5. Which man is accepted by God: the Pharisee or the tax collector?

The Oasis Activity

HELP THE KIDS AT THE TOP GO THROUGH
THE TOWN TO GET TO JESUS AND THEIR
FRIEND AT THE BOTTOM OF THE MAZE.

Lesson 19:
The Rich Ruler

Key Verse: Luke 19:10 (NIV)

For the Son of Man came to seek and save what was lost.

The Map:

Have you ever loved something so much that you didn't want to give it up? When I was young, I had a stuffed animal that I never wanted to get rid of! In this lesson, we are going to read about a man who didn't want to give something up to follow Jesus. Don't forget to start memorizing your next key verse. It is Luke 19:10.

The Dig: Luke 18:18-34

What question does the ruler ask Jesus?

What does Jesus tell him to do?

What does the ruler do? If you need a hint, look at verse 23.

What does Jesus tell His disciples is going to happen soon?

The Treasure:

You will never be sorry for following Jesus! The rich ruler thought his money would make him happier than following Jesus. He asked the right question about how to be saved, but he made the wrong decision by not giving up his money to follow Jesus.

The Display:

The rich ruler made the mistake of loving his money more than loving Jesus. What are some reasons why you love Jesus more than anything?

Lesson 20:
The Blind Beggar

Key Verse: Luke 19:10 (NIV)

For the Son of Man came to seek and save what was lost.

The Map:

One of my friends that I went to college with in Israel was blind. He learned to get around by using a walking stick. He did it, but it wasn't easy! In this lesson, we'll learn about a blind man that Jesus meets on the side of the road.

The Dig: Luke 18:35-43

Where is Jesus traveling?

What does the blind man ask Jesus to do?

What does Jesus do to help the blind man?

The rich ruler walks away from Jesus. What does the blind man do?

The Treasure:

Never stop praising Jesus! The blind beggar couldn't stop praising God for all that He had done for him. In verse 43, it says that other people saw him praising God and joined him!

The Display:

There is so much we can thank God for. The blind man praised God because he had been healed of his blindness. What are some things you can praise God for?

Lesson 21:
Zacchaeus

Key Verse: Luke 19:10 (NIV)

For the Son of Man came to seek and save what was lost.

The Map:

One year, while I was in the city of Jericho, I got food poisoning. I have never been so sick in my life! We're going to read about a man named Zacchaeus who lived in Jericho during the time of Jesus. He didn't need Jesus because he was sick, but because he needed to be forgiven. Let's dig!

The Dig: Luke 19:1-10

What is Zacchaeus' job?

Why is his job not liked by others?

How does Zacchaeus get to see Jesus?

What does Jesus say He wants to do?

What does Zacchaeus say he's going to do after Jesus leaves? If you need a hint, look at verse 8.

The Treasure:

Sinners are never beyond saving! Even though Zacchaeus had done some pretty bad things, God still loved him and was willing to forgive him. Zacchaeus knew that he wasn't living the way God wanted. He did the right thing by confessing his sin and turning to Jesus!

The Display:

Do you know what it means to confess? It means to admit when you have done something wrong. God wants us to admit when we have made a mistake because we are never beyond His love and forgiveness. What are some things you need to ask God to help you with right now?

Lesson 22:
Faithful Workers

Key Verse: Luke 19:10 (NIV)

For the Son of Man came to seek and save what was lost.

The Map:

When I was growing up, my parents gave me chores each week. When I did them each week, they rewarded me for my hard work! In this lesson, we are going to read a story Jesus tells in order to teach how we should always work hard for God.

The Dig: Luke 19:11-27

What do the people think is going to happen when Jesus gets to Jerusalem?

In Jesus' story, the king gives money to how many servants?

Do all of the servants work with the money the king gives them?

The Treasure:

Be faithful with the gifts God has given you! Jesus tells this story to show how each of us has different gifts and abilities that we can use for God. God wants us to use those gifts to serve Him and other people.

The Display:

Take a few minutes and discuss with your mom or dad the gifts that God has given you. God has created each of us special with different gifts to use to serve Him. What are yours?

Lesson 23:
Jesus Enters Jerusalem

Key Verse: Luke 19:10 (NIV)

For the Son of Man came to seek and save what was lost.

The Map:

In this lesson, we will be looking at what happens when Jesus enters Jerusalem. It won't be long until people will begin to see that He is heading there to die on the cross for the sins of the world. Let's dig!

The Dig: Luke 19:28-48

What does Jesus tell His disciples to get for him? Take a minute and read Zechariah 9:9.

When Jesus gets close to the Mount of Olives, what do the crowds start to do?

Why does Jesus weep, or cry, when He enters Jerusalem?

Once Jesus gets to Jerusalem, where does He go?

The Treasure:

Jesus is the King of Peace! He came riding in on a colt to show that He was the Messiah, or Savior, coming to save the world from their sins. He was coming to bring peace, but sadly, many people didn't want Him to be their Savior or King.

The Display:

Because Jesus is our Savior and King, we want to listen to Him and live for Him! How are some ways you show that Jesus is your King?

Lesson 24:
Jesus Questioned

Key Verse: Luke 19:10 (NIV)

For the Son of Man came to seek and save what was lost.

The Map:

I remember when I was in third grade and some students didn't let me sit at their lunch table the first day of school. Boy, was I sad! In this lesson, we're going to read about how Jesus was rejected by some of the Jewish leaders.

The Dig: Luke 20:1-19

In Jesus' parable, what does the man plant?

How many servants does the man send to bring back fruit from the vineyard?

Who does the owner finally send?

What do they do to the owner's son?

The Treasure:

God is patient! Jesus tells this story to show how God had sent the Jewish people many servants in the past. He was now sending them His Son, Jesus, to be their Savior. God kept giving them a chance to turn to Him to be forgiven. Unfortunately, some still didn't want to accept Him!

The Display:

I don't want to see any of my family or friends reject Jesus! We need to be patient and pray for friends who aren't Christians. Take a few minutes and list some friends or family you can pray for.

The Oasis

Congratulations! You have made it through the next six lessons! The Oasis is a chance to stop, rest up, and review what you have learned so far on the adventure. During each Oasis, you will be quizzed over the lessons you have already done. Do you think you can remember what you have studied so far? Let's find out!

Review Key Verse: Luke 19:10 (NIV)

Take a minute and tell your mom or dad the key verse. Remember, you are not allowed to look!

Review Questions:

1. What does Jesus ask the rich ruler to do?

2. What does the blind beggar do after Jesus heals him?

3. What does Zacchaeus promise to do after Jesus leaves his house?

4. Why does Jesus weep as He rides into Jerusalem?

5. How many servants are sent to the vineyard?

6. What do they do to the owner's son?

The Oasis Activity

LUKE 15:8-10

LUKE 15:11-32

LUKE 15:1-7

MATTHEW 13:45-46

2 CORINTHIANS 4:16-18

JOHN 3:16-17

"FOR THE SON OF MAN CAME TO SEEK AND TO SAVE THE LOST." LUKE 19:10

ZACCHAEUS CLIMBED A SYCAMORE TREE AND THE LORD SOUGHT HIM OUT.
CAN YOU SEEK AND FIND SOME OTHER ITEMS HIDDEN AMONGST THE LEAVES
AND FIGS WHICH THE BIBLE TELLS US MAY BE LOST OR NEED TO BE FOUND?

Lesson 25:
Give Yourself to God

Key Verse: Luke 20:25 (NIV)

He said to them, "Then give to Caesar what is Caesar's,
and to God what is God's."

The Map:

Has someone ever tried to trick you? What did they do? In this lesson, we are going to read about a time when the religious leaders tried to trick Jesus by asking Him a question. Let's take a look at what He says to them! Don't forget to start memorizing your next key verse. It is Luke 20:25.

The Dig: Luke 20:20-26

Who do the religious leaders send to Jesus?

What do they ask Him?

What does Jesus ask them for?

Whose image is on the coin?

Whose image are we made in? Take a look at Genesis 1:26-27.

The Treasure:

Give yourself to God! These religious leaders tried to trick Jesus, but it didn't work. They had a coin with Caesar's image on it. Jesus is reminding them that we are made in God's image and so therefore we belong to Him. The coin is Caesar's, but we belong to God!

The Display:

Because we belong to God, we want to spend our life obeying Him. What are some ways you show you belong to God?

Lesson 26:
God of the Living

Key Verse: Luke 20:25 (NIV)

He said to them, "Then give to Caesar what is Caesar's,
and to God what is God's."

The Map:

Just like the last lesson, we are going to read about how another group of religious leaders asks Jesus a question. This group did not believe in Heaven, the resurrection, or angels, but they are going to ask Jesus a question about what marriage is like in Heaven. Let's see what Jesus says!

The Dig: Luke 20:27-40

What group of religious leaders asks Jesus the question?

What do they ask Him about?

What does the word resurrection mean?

What does Jesus say won't happen in Heaven? If you need a hint, look at verse 36.

The Treasure:

Our God is alive! Jesus was teaching the Sadducees that Heaven is for real. They were asking about marriage, which showed they didn't really understand what Heaven is going to be like. People won't need to get married anymore. But most importantly, Jesus is teaching that there will no longer be any pain, sickness, or death. That will be pretty amazing!

The Display:

It's pretty hard to fully understand just how amazing Heaven will be! Take a few minutes and discuss what you think will be the best thing about Heaven.

Lesson 27:
Costly Love

Key Verse: Luke 20:25 (NIV)

He said to them, "Then give to Caesar what is Caesar's,
and to God what is God's."

The Map:

On one of my trips to Israel, we met a group of archaeologists who were selling fake treasure. These old pieces of pottery and coins looked real, but they weren't! I was not fooled! In this lesson, we're going to read about some religious leaders who looked like they loved God, but they really didn't. Let's dig!

The Dig: Luke 20:41 – 21:4

Who does Jesus say to beware of in this passage?

What does Jesus say they like to do?

Who does Jesus see putting two small coins in the offering?

Is Jesus pleased with her?

The Treasure:

You can't fake real faith! Jesus was upset at some of the religious leaders because they were only pretending to love God. Their actions didn't show real faith or love for God! Jesus was very pleased with the woman who gave the two small coins. No how matter how big or small, our actions show whether we really love God or not!

The Display:

Take a minute and go find two dimes. Once you have them, hold them in the palm of your hand. See how small they are? Did you know that the coins the widow gave were about half the size of a dime? They were really small! Because she didn't have very much money, it was a lot for her to give. What are big or small ways we show our faith in God?

Lesson 28:
Tough Times

Key Verse: Luke 20:25 (NIV)

He said to them, "Then give to Caesar what is Caesar's,
and to God what is God's."

The Map:

It's not always easy to be a Christian. Sometimes it's even dangerous! We are going to read about how Jesus taught His disciples to never give up, even when they faced tough times. Let's take a look at what Jesus says in this lesson.

The Dig: Luke 21:5-38

What does Jesus say is going to happen to the temple?

What are other signs Jesus mentions are going to happen?

What does Jesus tell His disciples not to do? Look again at verses 9 and 14.

The Treasure:

With God's help, we need to be strong! Jesus was warning His disciples that tough times were ahead. The temple was going to be destroyed, people were going to start being mean to them, and there would even be some people saying they were the Messiah or Savior. He wasn't trying to scare them; Jesus just wanted His disciples to be ready to stand firm no matter what!

The Display:

Sometimes it's not easy to be a Christian! I am thankful that we live in a country where we can go to church and be a Christian without fear, but not all Christians around the world can do that. Take some time and discuss with your mom or dad how you can "stand firm," but also pray for Christians in other parts of the world that may be facing tough times right now.

Lesson 29:
The Last Supper

Key Verse: Luke 20:25 (NIV)

He said to them, "Then give to Caesar what is Caesar's,
and to God what is God's."

The Map:

We are nearing the end of The Dig! These last few lessons are important because they tell us the story of how Jesus died and rose again for our sins. In this lesson, we'll see how Jesus is beginning to prepare His disciples for what is ahead.

The Dig: Luke 22:1-38

Name at least one of the disciples who is going to deny or betray Jesus.

The Passover was an important holiday for the Jewish people. It was a celebration of how God had saved them from their slavery in Egypt. God "passed over" or saved the Israelites if they sprinkled blood from a lamb on the doorframe of their home. What is Jesus teaching His disciples about Himself during this Passover meal?

Jesus' disciples want to know who is the greatest. How does Jesus teach His disciples to be great? For some help, look at verse 27.

The Treasure:

Jesus came to be a servant! He served us by being the perfect Passover Lamb. He was beginning to teach His disciples that He was going to die and rise again for the sins of the world. Some of His disciples would stick with Him, but others would not.

The Display:

Jesus was preparing His disciples about what was to come, but He was also teaching His disciples how to live until He returns. Being a servant means not just looking at your own wants or desires, but looking to help others. What are some ways you can be a servant to other people?

Lesson 30:
Your Will Be Done

Key Verse: Luke 20:25 (NIV)

He said to them, "Then give to Caesar what is Caesar's,
and to God what is God's."

The Map:

As much as I enjoy a good adventure, I do not enjoy flying in an airplane! Flying makes me pray a lot harder. We have already seen how Jesus was preparing His disciples about what was to come. Let's take a look at how Jesus prepared Himself. Let's dig!

The Dig: Luke 22:39-46

Where does Jesus go to pray?

Read verse 39 again. Depending on your Bible translation, it might say that Jesus went out to pray "as usual" or it was His "custom." What does that say about how often Jesus prayed?

What is Jesus praying about?

What are His disciples doing?

The Treasure:

Pray for what God wants, not just what you want! Sometimes we can ask God for the wrong things. Even though Jesus was troubled by the thought of going to the cross, He prayed that He would have the strength to do what God the Father wanted Him to do. He prayed, "Not my will, but yours, be done."

The Display:

Jesus' prayer is a great reminder of how we are to pray. We can be honest and tell God anything, but we should always remember to pray for God's will to be done in our life! How do you pray? Why do you think it's important to pray? What are some ways you can pray more often this week?

The Oasis

Congratulations! You have made it through the next six lessons! The Oasis is a chance to stop, rest up, and review what you have learned so far on the adventure. During each Oasis, you will be quizzed over the lessons you have already done. Do you think you can remember what you have studied so far? Let's find out!

Review Key Verse: Luke 20:25 (NIV)

Take a minute and tell your mom or dad the key verse. Remember, you are not allowed to look!

Review Questions:

1. Whose image is on the coin Jesus asks for?

2. Who does Jesus see putting two small coins in the offering?

3. What does Jesus say is going to happen to the temple?

4. How does Jesus teach His disciples to be great?

5. Where does Jesus go to pray?

6. What do Jesus' disciples do when He is praying?

The Oasis Activity

DENARIUS COIN

GOD DOES NOT PUT THE MOST IMPORTANT
THINGS ON THE OUTSIDE, BUT ON THE INSIDE.
WHAT CAN YOU DRAW TO SHOW HOW GOD
HAS MARKED YOU AS HIS ON THE INSIDE?

PEOPLE PUT PICTURES OF WHAT IS IMPORTANT TO
THEM ON THEIR COINS. DESIGN YOUR OWN COIN TO
SHOW WHAT IS IMPORTANT TO YOU.

YOUR COIN

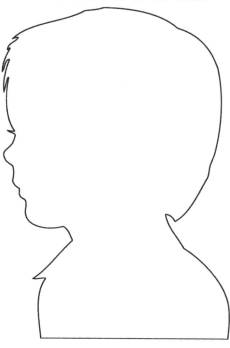

Lesson 31:
Jesus Arrested

Key Verses: Luke 24:33-34

And they rose that same hour and returned to Jerusalem. And they found the eleven and those who were with them gathered together, saying, "The Lord has risen indeed, and has appeared to Simon!"

The Map:

Several years ago, I went with a friend of mine who is a pastor to see someone in jail. The man we went to see was guilty of committing crimes that included stealing and doing drugs. Sadly, he was going to be in jail for a long time. In this lesson, we'll see what happens to Jesus even though He was innocent and without any sin. Don't forget to start memorizing your next key verses. They are Luke 24:33-34.

The Dig: Luke 22:47-71

What happens to Jesus at the beginning of this passage?

Who comes to arrest him?

What does Peter do when a girl asks if he is a disciple?

What do the guards do to Jesus?

The Treasure:

Jesus suffered unfairly! Though Jesus was arrested and mistreated, He was innocent. People did not want to receive Him as their Savior and so they rejected Jesus. Even though He was unfairly arrested, God was showing us how He was going to lovingly save us.

The Display:

Jesus never fought back with hurtful words or weapons. He continued to trust God the Father and love those who were mistreating Him. How do you show love for those who are mean to you? Are there ways you can show love to people who aren't always nice?

Lesson 32:
Crucify Him

Key Verses: Luke 24:33-34

And they rose that same hour and returned to Jerusalem. And they found the eleven and those who were with them gathered together, saying, "The Lord has risen indeed, and has appeared to Simon!"

The Map:

The first year my wife and I were married, we received a letter telling us how much we owed for a repair on our house. It was very expensive and we were worried because we didn't know how we were going to afford it. In this lesson, we are going to read about how Jesus paid a debt we could never have paid. Let's dig!

The Dig: Luke 23:1-49

What do the religious leaders accuse Jesus of? For a hint, see verse 2.

What are the crowds yelling?

Who is crucified next to Jesus?

What does Jesus say to God the Father as He is on the cross?

The Treasure:

Jesus paid our debt! Our sin separates us from God. Because of our sin, we owe God a debt we could never pay back on our own. But because God loves us, He was willing to pay the price of our sins for us. Jesus died on the cross to take our place and pay the price of our sins so we could be forgiven. That is amazing love!

The Display:

It is amazing to think about all that Jesus suffered and went through for us. Tonight before you go to bed, I want you to write a letter to Jesus thanking Him for all He has done for you. When you're done, put your note or letter in a place that you will see every day. This will be a great reminder of God's love.

Lesson 33:
He Is Alive

Key Verses: Luke 24:33-34

And they rose that same hour and returned to Jerusalem. And they found the eleven and those who were with them gathered together, saying, "The Lord has risen indeed, and has appeared to Simon!"

The Map:

If the story of Jesus stopped with His death, it would be a pretty sad story. But the good news is that is not how the story ends! In this lesson, we are going to read what God does shortly after Jesus was crucified for our sins.

The Dig: Luke 23:50 – 24:35

Who takes Jesus' body and places Him in a tomb?

Who are the first people to discover that Jesus is alive?

Who else is at Jesus' empty tomb?

What happens to the two men walking to Emmaus?

The Treasure:

Jesus is alive! Jesus not only died for our sins, but God raised Him from the dead! This proved that Jesus really was the Messiah, or Savior, of the whole world. The Bible promises something really amazing: Everyone who believes in Jesus will someday be with Him and one another in Heaven. That is good news!

The Display:

Take a moment and read John 3:16. Has there ever been a time that you have told Jesus you believe in Him and you want to live for Him? If not, take a moment and pray with your mom or dad. Tell Jesus you believe He died and rose again for you and you want to live for Him. If you have already done this, take some time right now to pray for friends or family who aren't Christians. And don't forget to keep praying for them!

Lesson 34:
Tell the World

Key Verses: Luke 24:33-34

And they rose that same hour and returned to Jerusalem. And they found the eleven and those who were with them gathered together, saying, "The Lord has risen indeed, and has appeared to Simon!"

The Map:

It's hard to believe, but this is the final lesson of Luke. You made it! But as we'll see, the story doesn't end here. In this final lesson, let's read what Jesus wants His disciples to do up until He returns. Let's dig!

The Dig: Luke 24:36-53

How do Jesus' disciples react when He comes to see them?

What does He tell them to do to prove He is really alive?

Who does Jesus promise He is going to send to them very shortly? See Acts 1:4, 8.

Once the Holy Spirit gives them power, what are they supposed to go do?

The Treasure:

Go be a witness! Jesus promised that He was going to send the Holy Spirit to live in us and give us the power we need to live for God. Jesus wants us to spread this amazing news that God loves us and wants us to have a relationship with Him.

The Display:

Even though we are done studying the gospel of Luke, God is not done with us! He wants us to live our lives to please Him. One of the ways we do this is by telling others about Jesus. How can you tell others about Jesus?

Congratulations on completing Luke Volume 2! I hope you join me on another Bible adventure soon. Until then, keep your eyes on Jesus!

The Oasis

Congratulations! You have made it to the last Oasis! As you know, the Oasis is a chance to stop, rest up, and review what you have learned so far on the adventure. Do you think you can remember what you have studied so far? Let's find out!

Review Key Verses: Luke 24:33-34

Take a minute and tell your mom or dad the key verses. Remember, you are not allowed to look!

Review Questions:

1. Who arrests Jesus?

2. What do they do to Him after He is arrested?

3. What are the crowds shouting?

4. What does Jesus say to those who have Him crucified?

5. Who finds Jesus' empty tomb first?

6. Who tells the women that Jesus has risen?

7. What do Jesus' disciples do when He appears to them?

8. What does He tell His disciples to go do?

The Oasis Activity

AND THEY ROSE THAT SAME HOUR AND RETURNED TO JERUSALEM. AND THEY FOUND THE ELEVEN AND THOSE WHO WERE WITH THEM GATHERED TOGETHER, SAYING, "THE LORD HAS RISEN INDEED, AND HAS APPEARED TO SIMON!" LUKE 24:33-34

1 _ _ _ _ _   _ _ _ _ _   4 _ _ _ _   7 _ _ _ _ _ _ _   10 _ _ _ _ _
2 _ _ _ _ _ _   5 _ _ _ _ _ _   8 _ _ _ _ _ _ _   11 _ _ _ _ _
3 _ _ _ _ _   6 _ _ _ _ _ _ _ _ _   9 _ _ _ _ _

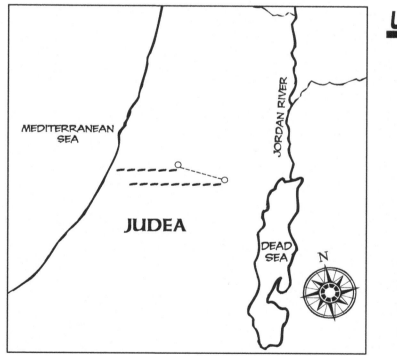

UNSCRAMBLE

- ☐ SJMAE
- ☐ WADNRE
- ☐ LEJREUMSA
- ☐ HTAMTEW
- ☐ MUASME
- ☐ EAMJS
- ☐ DASUJ
- ☐ SAMHOT
- ☐ NSOMI
- ☐ LTORHOMWEAB
- ☐ OMSNI EERPT
- ☐ ONJH
- ☐ IPPLIH

UNSCRAMBLE THE WORDS TO FIND THE NAMES OF THE 11 DISCIPLES AND THE 2 LOCATIONS ON THE MAP.

(HINT: THE NAMES OF ALL THE DISCIPLES IS LISTED IN LUKE 6:14-16)

In Closing

Congratulations!

You have finished Luke Volume 2. I hope you continue to enjoy reading and studying the Bible as much as I do. The Bible is not just any normal book. It is God's Word, but it is also God's Story!

The Bible tells us how in the beginning God created the heavens and the earth. Everything and everyone belongs to Him! God created us to live in a loving friendship and relationship with Him. The bad news is that just like Adam and Eve, our sins separate us from God. But the good news is that because God loves us, He sent us a Savior, Jesus, to rescue us from our sins.

John 3:16 says, "For God so loved the world, that he gave his only Son, that whoever believes in him should not perish but have eternal life." The news is that good! When we believe in Jesus, God forgives us of our sins and gives us everlasting life! As Christians, we do not go through life alone. We know that God loves us and is always with us no matter what happens. And best of all, some day we will be together in Heaven with God. Now that is something to look forward to!

I hope you will continue reading and studying God's Word. But most importantly, I pray that as you learn more about God it will help you to love God more. He is truly amazing and worth living for!

There is a lot more to dig for, so be sure to check out another Bible adventure soon!

Happy Digging,

Doc

Key Terms

Angel: Angels were created by God to be helpers or messengers. They do not have a physical body, but are created, spiritual beings.

Chief Priests: These were a group of Jewish leaders who served as priests in the Temple.

Christ (or Messiah): Christ, or Messiah, means God's anointed or chosen savior. This is Jesus!

Demons: These are bad or evil angels who sinned against God and who now work against God in the world.

Fast (or Fasting): A fast is when someone does not eat and instead focuses on prayer, repentance, and the study of God's Word. Before, and even during the time of Jesus, the Jewish people fasted during the biblical holidays. They would often fast and pray for forgiveness, for God to come and save them, and when they were sad. A fast could last a day, several days, or even several weeks!

Holy Spirit: The Holy Spirit is not just a power or force. He is God, by His power and presence, living in us as Christians. The Bible teaches that God the Father, Jesus, and the Holy Spirit all work together as One.

King Herod: Herod was the King over Judea during the time of Jesus' birth.

Leprosy: Leprosy was a skin disease that caused the Israelites to be unclean according to God's commandments in the Old Testament book of Leviticus. An Israelite with leprosy had to move out of the camp until they were clean.

Pharisees: These people were a group of Jews during Jesus' time who were very concerned with obeying God's commandments. They believed God had given Moses all of these commandments at Mt. Sinai to write for all of the Jewish people to obey. These commandments were called the Written Law and are the first five books of the Old Testament. Not only did they believe God gave Moses these commandments to write down, but they also believed that God spoke other commandments to them that they called the Oral Law. Eventually the Oral Law was written down in a book that is now today called the Mishnah.

Repent (or Repentance): Repent means to turn away from sin and turn to God.

Sabbath: Sabbath means "to cease." The Sabbath is a weekly day of rest. It runs from sunset on Friday to sunset on Saturday. It is a special day each week to cease from working and focus on worshipping God.

Sadducees: This was a group of Jewish leaders during the time of Jesus. Most scholars believe they helped to run the Temple in Jerusalem. They had slightly different beliefs than the Pharisees. For example, they only accepted the first five books of the Old Testament, the Written Law, as God's Word. Unlike the Pharisees, they did not believe in the resurrection of the dead, or in angels (Mark 12:18; Acts 23:8).

Satan (or the Devil): Satan, or the Devil, is the leader of all fallen and bad angels.

The Temple: The Temple was a large building, like a church, where the Jewish people worshipped God. It was located in Jerusalem.

About the Author

 Patrick Schwenk is a husband, father, and pastor. He is married to Ruth Schwenk, the creator of *The Better Mom* (www.thebettermom.com). They met while attending the Moody Bible Institute in Chicago, Illinois. Pat and his wife have been married for fourteen years and currently have four children ages three to ten.

For additional information on parenting and discipleship resources, visit www.thedigforkids.com and www.thebettermom.com.

Contact Info:

Facebook: Pat Schwenk

Twitter: @patschwenk

The Dig: www.thedigforkids.com

Email: thedigforkids@gmail.com

Design and Artwork:

Cover Design by Design by Insight – www.DesignByInsight.net

Oasis Artwork by Steve Miller – www.torchbearerstudios.com

Edited by Jordy Liz Edits – www.jordylizedits.com

Made in the USA
Las Vegas, NV
17 April 2022

47591531R10044